THE STORY OF THE LOS ANGELES CLIPPERS

Bob McAdoo

Reggie Jackson

A HISTORY OF HOOPS

THE STORY OF THE

LOS ANGELES CLIPPERS

JIM WHITING

Blake Griffin

CREATIVE EDUCATION / CREATIVE PAPERBACKS

Published by Creative Education and Creative Paperbacks
P.O. Box 227, Mankato, Minnesota 56002
Creative Education and Creative Paperbacks are imprints of
The Creative Company
www.thecreativecompany.us

Design and production by Blue Design (www.bluedes.com)
Art direction by Rita Marshall
Production layout by Rachel Klimpel and Ciara Beitlich

Photographs by AP Images (Kenny Ignelzi, Kim Klement, Kirby Lee, Brian
Rothmuller/Icon Sportswire, Mark J. Terrill, Elaine Thompson), Corbis, Ebay
(bigrocx-auction), Getty (Bettmann, Kevorak Djansezian, Stephen Dunn,
Garrett Ellwood, Focus On Sport, Sean Gardner, Adam Glanzman, George
Gojkovich, Noah Graham, Scott Halleran, Soobum Im, Josh Lefkowitz, John
W. McDonough, Mike Powell, Rick Stewart, Jared C. Tilton), Newscom (John
Angelillo/UPI), Shutterstock (Brocreative, Andrey Burmakin, Valentin Valkov)

Library of Congress Cataloging-in-Publication Data
Names: Whiting, Jim, 1943- author.
Title: The story of the Los Angeles Clippers / by Jim Whiting.
Description: Mankato, Minnesota : Creative Education/Creative Paperbacks,
   2023. | Series: Creative Sports. A History of Hoops | Includes index. |
   Audience: Ages 8-12 | Audience: Grades 4-6 | Summary: "Middle grade
   basketball fans are introduced to the extraordinary history of NBA's L.A.
   Clippers with a photo-laden narrative of their greatest successes and
   losses"-- Provided by publisher.
Identifiers: LCCN 2022009498 (print) | LCCN 2022009499 (ebook) | ISBN
   9781640266292 (library binding) | ISBN 9781682771853 (paperback) | ISBN
   9781640007703 (ebook)
Subjects: LCSH: Los Angeles Clippers (Basketball team)--History--Juvenile
   literature.
Classification: LCC GV885.52.L65 W55 2023 (print) | LCC GV885.52.L65 (ebook)
   | DDC 796.323/640979494--dc23/eng/20220224
LC record available at https://lccn.loc.gov/2022009498
LC ebook record available at https://lccn.loc.gov/2022009499

Chris Paul

CONTENTS

LEGENDS OF THE HARDWOOD

Terance Mann

8

"MANN"ING UP

The Los Angeles Clippers faced the Utah Jazz in the 2020–21 National Basketball Association (NBA) Western Conference semifinals. The Clippers had the weight of their 50-year history pressing down on them. They had never advanced beyond this point to compete in the conference finals before. It was the longest streak of futility in league history.

The Jazz had taken the first two games. Los Angeles battled back to win the next two as superstar small forward Kawhi Leonard poured in 65 points. But he suffered a knee injury at the end of Game 4. He couldn't play anymore in the postseason. Many sports teams have a motto for dealing with injuries: "next man up." It means that a bench player is thrust into a starting role. For the Clippers it was "next Mann up." Leonard's replacement was Terance Mann. He had only scored 12 points during the first four games. He scored 13 points as a starter in Game 5 as the Clippers clawed out a narrow win. His three-point shot opened the Clippers' scoring in Game 6. But they fell behind 75–50 as the third quarter began.

At that point, Mann took over. "I just had to lock in and do what I had to do," said Mann. "They were leaving me open." He scored 20 points during the rest of the quarter. That helped cut the Utah lead to just 3 points at 94–91. Los Angeles took a narrow lead early in the final quarter. Mann's five points several minutes later keyed a 9–0 run that put the game away. The Clippers won 131–119. Mann finished with 39 points. It was his highest point total since high school. With the outcome assured, coach Tyronn Lue called a timeout to substitute for Mann. The fans gave him a thundering standing ovation. ESPN's Rachel Nichols said that "this night will forever be known as 'The Terance Mann Game.'"

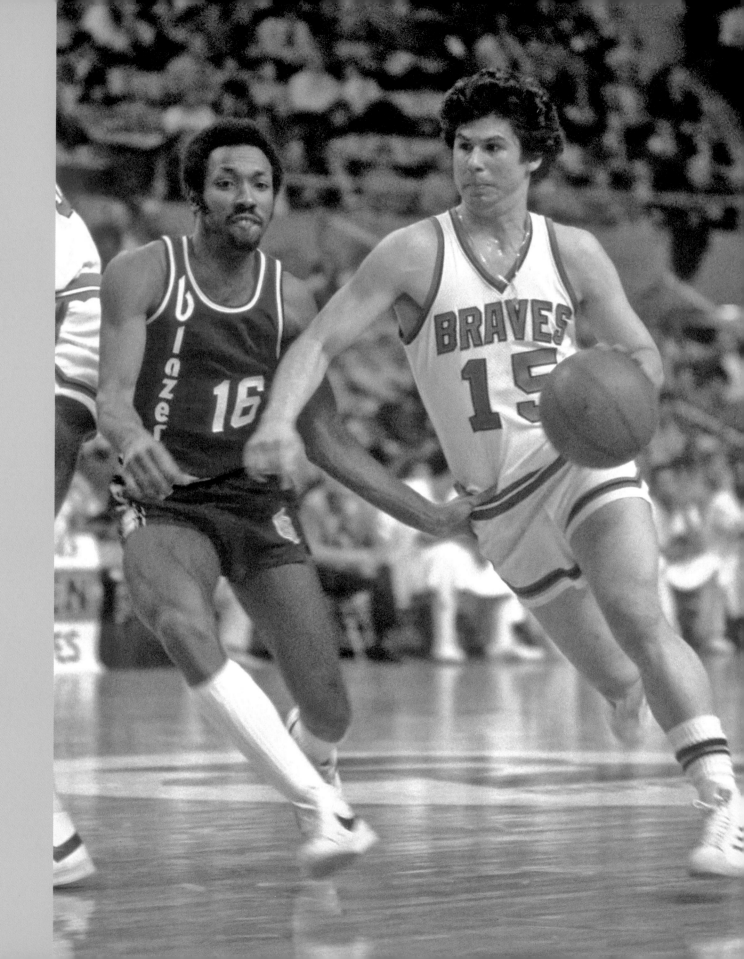

TRANSCONTINENTAL TREK

BRAVES
JOHN HUMMER

The Clippers' story began in 1970 on the opposite side of the country. The NBA was enjoying increasing popularity. The league decided to expand. It granted franchises to Portland, Oregon; Cleveland, Ohio; and Buffalo, New York. Buffalo team officials chose Braves as the new team's name. They wanted to honor the region's American Indian heritage.

The Braves received several players from other teams. They also participated in the 1970 NBA Draft. Many fans wanted them to select Calvin Murphy. He was a 5-foot-9 point guard from nearby Niagara University. He had averaged 33 points a game in college. Instead, Buffalo chose forward/center John Hummer of Princeton University. Murphy went elsewhere and had a Hall-of-Fame career. Hummer averaged just over eight points per game in three seasons in Buffalo. This was the first of many confusing personnel moves the team made during its history. The Braves struggled to a 22–60 mark. They posted similar records the following two years.

Fortunately, Buffalo's draft choices improved. They took shooting guard/small forward Randy Smith in 1971. At training camp, coach Dolph Schayes watched Smith easily outpace his teammates during a series of drills. "He's fast," Schayes said. "He's staying." Smith would go on to average nearly 18

Ernie DeGregorio

LEGENDS
OF THE HARDWOOD

RANDY SMITH
SHOOTING GUARD/SMALL FORWARD
HEIGHT: 6-FOOT-3
BRAVES/CLIPPERS SEASONS 1971–79, 1982–83

GOOOOOOOALLLLLL!

Randy Smith was a gifted athlete. He led his
college basketball team to three straight league
championships. He high-jumped 6 feet, 10 inches.
Above all, he was a soccer All-American. "If all things
had been equal, I probably would have chosen soccer,"
Smith said. "That's what I was gearing for, but the
average salary of a soccer player is $10,000. The
average NBA salary is $105,000. I didn't have a choice."
Soccer was still in his blood during his early hoops
career. He tried out with the Tampa Bay Rowdies of
the North American Soccer League in 1975. The team
offered him a contract. The Braves wouldn't let him
accept it. He tried twice more in later years. He was cut
both times. He'd been away from soccer too long.

Randy Smith

points a game with the team. In 1972, the Braves chose power forward/center Bob McAdoo. He was named NBA Rookie of the Year. Buffalo added point guard Ernie DiGregorio in the 1973 NBA Draft. He also became NBA Rookie of the Year. These additions helped Buffalo make the playoffs that season. They lost in the first round. The same thing happened in the following season. The Braves went 46–36 in 1975–76. They won their first-ever playoff series. But they lost in the second round.

The wheels started coming off in 1976–77. Buffalo traded McAdoo. They obtained future Hall-of-Famer Moses Malone only to trade him after just two games. Like Murphy, he would become a star with other teams. Small forward Adrian Dantley became the third Braves player in five years to be named NBA Rookie of the Year. He was traded at the end of the season. The team plunged to 30 wins. It managed just 27 in 1977–78.

The Braves' dismal record kept fans away. That set the stage for an unusual change of ownership. Movie producer Ira Levin had purchased the Boston Celtics in 1972. He lived in California. He wanted to move the team there. The NBA would never allow that. Few teams in professional sports are so closely identified with their home cities. Levin approached Buffalo owner John Y. Brown. He offered to swap franchises with him. Brown knew the Celtics were much more popular than the Braves. He agreed to the deal.

Levin moved the Braves to San Diego. He changed their name to Clippers. Clippers were graceful sailing ships. They sailed across the Pacific Ocean from San Diego and nearby ports during the nineteenth century.

The "Clips," as people began calling them, were led by shooting guard Lloyd Free. (He soon changed his name to World B. Free.) In 1978–79, he averaged nearly 29 points a game, taking shots from seemingly impossible angles. "People come right out of their seats when I do my thing," Free boasted. "They like seeing guys taking crazy shots and hitting them." San Diego sailed to a 43–39 record. It wasn't good enough to make the playoffs. Smith was traded after the season. Free averaged 30 points a game in 1979–80. Then the Clippers traded him, too.

In 1981, attorney Donald Sterling bought the team. San Diego won just 17 games that season. Rookie forward Tom Chambers was one of the few bright spots. He led the team with 17 points a game. The team selected Terry Cummings in the 1982 NBA Draft. He was named NBA Rookie of the Year. Both players were gone after the 1983–84 season.

World B. Free

Terry Cummings

LOS ANGELES CLIPPERS

DRAFT DAY DISASTERS

In the 1982 NBA Draft, the Clippers chose power forward Terry Cummings. He became NBA Rookie of the Year. In 2003, the Clippers chose center Chris Kaman. He became an All-Star. In the 21 years in between, the Clippers had only one top draft pick who became a solid performer. That was power forward Danny Manning in 1988. He averaged 19 points a game in his six seasons in Los Angeles. The others were busts. A few did play well—after the Clippers traded them. During those two decades of poor draft choices, the Clippers had a single winning season. No other NBA team has had such a dismal streak.

SECOND FIDDLE IN LOS ANGELES

Sterling publicly said he would keep the Clippers in San Diego. But he really wanted to move them to Los Angeles, where he lived. The NBA already had a successful franchise in Los Angeles, the Lakers. Sterling moved them anyway in 1984. He didn't ask the league's permission. The NBA fined him $6 million.

The Clippers won only 31 games the first season in their new city. Rookie power forward Michael Cage became an instant fan favorite for his ferocious rebounding. The Clippers won 32 games in the second season. Then they plummeted to 17 wins in 1987–88. The team chose power forward Danny Manning in the 1988 NBA Draft. He had been College Player of the Year. He was hurt most of the year. The Clippers went 21–61. After two more losing seasons, the Clippers finally found success in 1991–92. They won 45 games and slipped into the playoffs for the first time in 16 years. It had been the longest postseason drought in NBA history. They lost in the first round to the Utah Jazz, 3 games to 2. A 41–41 record the following year was good enough for another playoff appearance. The Houston Rockets sank them in the first round.

The Clippers returned to their losing ways the following season … and the one after that … and so on. The Clippers hit bottom in the lockout-shortened 1998–99 season. They scraped together just 9 wins while losing 41. Only the Vancouver

Danny Manning

Grizzlies, with eight, had fewer wins. The Clips attracted the fewest fans in the league. In 1999, the team moved into the Staples Center. The arena was also the Lakers' home. The two teams went in opposite directions. The Lakers won the NBA championship. The Clippers finished with a league-worst 15–67 mark. In 2001, though, the Clippers added some much-needed star power. They traded for power forward Elton Brand. "Brand gives us more rebounding," said Clippers general manager Elgin Baylor. "He's a good shot blocker and can run the floor also." It didn't matter. The Clippers continued losing.

Things started to turn around in 2004–05. The Clippers had a better record (37–45) than the Lakers (34–48). They built on that momentum the following season. The Clippers won their first playoff series in 30 years. They beat the Denver Nuggets, 4 games to 1. They nearly topped the Phoenix Suns in the second round before losing, 4 games to 3.

SAILING TOWARD THE TOP

The Clippers slid backward for the next five years. The low point came in 2008–09 when they won just 19 games. But the team was setting a course for better days. In 2008, the Clippers had drafted center DeAndre Jordan. He recorded 10 dunks in a single game. Only two other players had ever done that. The Clips drafted power forward Blake Griffin the following year. He suffered a knee injury and missed the entire season but bounced back in 2010–11. He was named NBA Rookie of the Year and played in the All-Star Game "I think it's been a while since there's been a rookie as good as him," teammate Chris Kaman said.

DeAndre Jordan

LEGENDS
OF THE HARDWOOD

MICHAEL CAGE
POWER FORWARD
HEIGHT: 6-FOOT-9
CLIPPERS SEASONS: 1984–88

KING OF THE BOARDS

Michael Cage was nicknamed "Windexman." The name refers to the famous window-cleaning product. His rebounding ability was often referred to as "cleaning the glass." In the last game of the 1987–88 season, Cage needed 28 rebounds to win the league rebounding title. "At the end of the third quarter, I had 19 rebounds," Cage said, "but I was exhausted. I had nothing left in the tank." Somehow he snared 11 rebounds in the final quarter. He finished with 30. It was his last game as a Clipper. He became yet another great player the Clippers traded away.

Before the 2011–12 season, Los Angeles had just six winning seasons during their 41-year history. Many people called them the "Paper Clips" because they were so consistently bad. Team officials decided to do something dramatic. They traded four players for superstar point guard Chris Paul of the New Orleans Hornets. "We decided for a player of Chris's caliber that it was just time to make the move and push all our chips into the center of the table," said Clippers official Neil Olshey. "He's a warrior, and he's going to take this whole organization to the next level." He became the first Clipper named to the All-NBA First Team. The Clippers surged to 40–26 in the lockout-shortened 2011–12 season. Its winning percentage of .606 was the best in team history to that point. The Clippers defeated the Memphis Grizzlies in the opening round of the playoffs. It was just their third-ever playoff series win. The San Antonio Spurs swept them in the second round.

That season was just the start. Fans enjoyed watching Paul's high looping passes to Jordan, Griffin, and other teammates. They began to refer to the team as "Lob City." ESPN sportswriter Arash Markazi said, "Like most good nicknames, it eventually took on a life of its own, and the Clippers are living up to it on a nightly basis, with lob dunks so spectacular they instantly become trending topics on Twitter." The Clippers had a 25–6 mark at the end of December in the 2012–13 season, the best in the NBA. It included a team-best 17-game winning streak. They finished 56–26, their best record in history. The Clippers took a 2–0 lead over the Memphis Grizzlies in the first round of the playoffs. Unfortunately, Griffin sprained his ankle during practice and was sidelined. The Grizzlies won the next four games.

Griffin returned to form in the 2013–14 season. The Clippers added seasoned veterans such as shooting guards J.J. Redick and Jamal Crawford. Lob City sailed to 57 wins. They defeated the Golden State Warriors in the first round of the playoffs, 4 games to 3. They couldn't get past Oklahoma City in the next round, though.

ELTON BRAND

POWER FORWARD

HEIGHT: 6-FOOT-8

CLIPPERS SEASONS: 2001–2008

MAKING A BETTER BRAND

In 2005–06, the Clippers won 47 games. It was their best record
in 31 years. One of the main reasons was Elton Brand. The
Chicago Bulls had made him the first overall pick in the 1999 NBA
Draft even though many people thought he was undersized for a
power forward. They traded him to the Clippers two years later.
In 2005–06, he had the best season of his career. He averaged
nearly 25 points, 10 rebounds, and 2.5 blocked shots a game.
No player his height has matched that stat line. Some people
thought he should be the league's MVP. He wasn't, but he did
win the Joe Dumars Sportsmanship Award. It was especially
meaningful because the players vote to determine the winner.

NEW SKIPPER FOR THE CLIPPERS

icrosoft multi-billionaire Steve Ballmer bought the team before the 2014–15 season. He pledged to "do everything in my power to ensure the Clippers continue to win—and win big—in Los Angeles." The team went 56–26 in the following season. They defeated San Antonio in the first round of the playoffs. The Clippers took a 3–1 series lead over Houston in the next round. But the Rockets won three games in a row to take the series.

The Clippers returned to the playoffs in 2015–16 with 53 wins. Unfortunately, Griffin and Paul were both injured. The Portland Trail Blazers bounced them out in the first round. The following season was similar. Once again, the Clippers were in the playoffs. Once again, they lost in the first round, this time to the Utah Jazz.

The Clippers traded Paul before the following season. Griffin left at the mid-way point. Los Angeles fell to 42–40 and missed the playoffs for the first time in seven years. Jordan moved on as well. The Clippers still managed to make the playoffs in 2018–19. They lost to the Golden State Warriors in the first round.

DONALD STERLING
OWNER
CLIPPERS SEASONS: 1981–2014

L O S   A N G E L E S   C L I P P E R S

WORST. OWNER. EVER?

In 2000, *Sports Illustrated* ran a story about the Clippers. It was titled "The Worst Franchise in Sports History." The story blamed owner Donald Sterling for the team's misfortunes. "I'll build the Clippers through the draft, free agency, trades, spending whatever it takes to make a winner," Sterling said when he bought the team. None of that was true. He often delayed paying his players. He asked coach Paul Silas to serve as team trainer. Every other team had a separate trainer. Nothing changed when the team moved to Los Angeles. In 2014, recordings of Sterling making racist comments became public. Players threatened to boycott Clippers' games. The NBA made him sell the team

Micro

STEVE BALLMER
OWNER
CLIPPERS SEASONS:
2014–PRESENT

TAKING A DIFFERENT PATH

Microsoft co-founders Bill Gates and Paul Allen were computer experts at a relatively young age. Not Steve Ballmer. He studied economics and mathematics at Harvard University, where he met Gates. He briefly worked for Procter and Gamble as a product manager. He entered Stanford University's MBA program but dropped out when Gates hired him as business manager for the then-new Microsoft Corporation. Ballmer received a salary and shares of Microsoft stock. He became the company's chief executive officer in 2000 and served for 14 years before retiring and buying the Clippers. He has been the richest major sports team owner since then. According to *Forbes* magazine, he is among the wealthiest men in the world. His net worth is over $90 billion.

Los Angeles added a pair of superstars for the 2019–20 season: two-time NBA Defensive Player of the Year small forward Kawhi Leonard and seven-time All-Star swingman Paul George. They won 49 games in the COVID-shortened season. They were the second seed in the playoffs, the highest in team history. But after taking a 3-1 series lead over the Denver Nuggets in the conference semifinals, they couldn't close it out.

The lingering effects of the COVID-19 pandemic caused a late start to the 2020–21 season, resulting in 10 fewer games. The Clippers won 47 games. They beat the Dallas Mavericks, 4 games to 3, in the first round of the playoffs. Then they upset the Jazz. For the first time in team history, they were in the conference finals. They faced Phoenix and Chris Paul, who had joined the Suns that season. Phoenix won the first game. The Suns took the second by a single point on a field goal with seven-tenths of a second left. The Clippers won Game 3. They lost Game 4 by four points after missing 12 fourth-quarter shots that would have tied the score or given them the lead. They won Game 5 to stay alive. The Suns crushed them in Game 6 as Paul poured in 41 points against his former teammates. Phoenix won the series, 4–2.

Before the 2021-22 season, Ballmer broke ground for a new arena called the Intuit Dome, scheduled to open in 2024. It will cost a reported $2 billion, the same

Paul George

as the purchase price for the team in 2014. "We needed to say, 'We're our own guys. We don't play in the same place as the other guys,'" he said. "We're going to build our own building, more of our own identity, more of our own personality."

That may have been the best news from the 2021–22 season. Leonard's injury from the previous postseason kept him out for the entire year. George injured an elbow and missed 51 games. Without them, the team struggled. The Clippers played the entire season within a few games on either side of the .500 mark. George returned late in the season and helped the Clippers finish 42–40. But he missed the second play-in game for the playoffs due to illness. Los Angeles lost to the Timberwolves 109–104 and the Pelicans 105–101. They missed the playoffs. The Clippers hope to get a boost in hopes of returning to postseason play. In the offseason, they signed five-time All-Star guard John Wall. He's averaged over 19 points and 9 assists per game in his 10-year career.

The Los Angeles Clippers have finally developed a solid core of players. The "Paper Clips" era has ended. The team's fans hope to "clip" an NBA championship banner to the rafters of the new Intuit Dome someday soon.

Kawhi Leonard

INDEX

Corey Maggette